Haul Away!

Teambuilding Lessons from a Voyage Around Cape Horn

by
Rob Duncan

authorHOUSE™

1663 LIBERTY DRIVE, SUITE 200
BLOOMINGTON, INDIANA 47403
(800) 839-8640
WWW.AUTHORHOUSE.COM

© 2005 Rob Duncan. All Rights Reserved.

No part of this book may be reproduced, stored in a retrieval system, or transmitted by any means without the written permission of the author.

First published by AuthorHouse 03/08/05

ISBN: 1-4208-3032-5 (sc)

Printed in the United States of America
Bloomington, Indiana

This book is printed on acid-free paper.

Table of Contents

Foreword ix

Chapter 1: The Need for a Quest 1

Chapter 2: Casting Off 10

Chapter 3: Out of Sight of Land 22

Chapter 4: Steady as she Goes 37

Chapter 5: First Landfall 47

Chapter 6: Casting Off Again 58

Chapter 7: The Worst Place on Earth 69

Chapter 8: Journey's End 83

Chapter 9: Epilogue 90

Appendix One: On Being a Leader 97

Appendix Two: Motivational Teambuilding Seminars by Rob Duncan 102

For Tracy,
and in memory of my parents Douglas and Elizabeth

Haul away your bowline, our ship she is a-rolling
Oh, haul away your bowline, your bowline haul!

Haul away your bowline, our skipper he's a-growling,
Oh, haul away your bowline, your bowline haul!

From "Haul Away Your Bowline", in The Grieg-Duncan Folk Song Collection George Innis, (1905)

Foreword

It is 10:58pm, ship's time, on November 19th, 2002, and we are directly below Cape Horn. I am standing alone on the portside deck, near the bow of the ship. I can see the dark pyramid-shaped mass of the great landmark with its lonely lights on either side of the peak. I remove the gold diamond stud in my left ear that has been keeping a place for my Cape Horn earring. I toss the stud as far as I can into the ocean toward the Horn: "This is for you, King Neptune, for good luck in case I come down here again."

I have been superstitious about not trying on my Cape Horn gold hoop until this very moment. After a few minutes of fumbling, it is in place. It feels heavy and huge; it feels appropriate. After years of reading and dreaming about rounding the Horn – this most dangerous place in the world for sailors, this graveyard of some 800 ships and 10,000 sailors – I am finally here.

The seas are rolling behind us, around 30 feet high or more, and we are rocketing along at almost 10 knots with plenty of sails up. The winds are with us, pushing us around this deadly landmark. Soon we will be able to make the fabled left turn up into the Atlantic Ocean. But I am not done throwing things into the sea here.

I have been carrying 2 extra gold earrings in my kitbag. One is in memory of Harry Mitchell, a sailor who died at the age of 70, in a single-handed, round-the-world sailing race in the late 1995. His dream had been to round Cape Horn, and he had died not far from here – nobody ever found out what happened, but most likely his small sailboat was simply overwhelmed by the huge seas and storms down here. I recall him being interviewed in a documentary film about the race. He spoke about wanting to wear the gold earring in his left ear, the age-old symbol of the Cape Horner, of being able to say "I've been there; I've done it". The other earring I brought with me was in honor of Gerry Roufs, who died in another single-handed, round-the-world race in 1997. Gerry had also been lost, just short of rounding Cape Horn. I found Gerry's story inspiring, because he had taken a risk in midlife – abandoning a law career in Canada to move to France to pursue serious distance sailboat racing. For each of these men, I toss a Cape Horner's gold earring into the sea, one for Harry and one for Gerry, as a way of thanking them both for the inspiration. After my simple tribute, I go back down to the deckhouse to join the party, the Cape Horners' party.

In September 2002, I left the relative comfort and security of a college teaching position to follow a dream of rounding Cape Horn under sail. I flew to San Diego from my hometown of Vancouver, and hopped on board the bark *Europa* as a deckhand. The vessel, a square-rigged tall ship first commissioned in 1911, was to be my home for 75 days as we sailed from San Diego to Easter Island, then around Cape Horn into the Falkland Islands, a distance of 8,000 miles. Over the course of the voyage, I grew from a terrified novice into a confident, competent sailor, as comfortable as a person can be in 40-foot waves, and Southern Ocean storm conditions. Along the way we, the crew, grew from a barely functioning assortment of disparate individuals into a highly functioning, deeply bonded team. Together we were able to accomplish what no one of us could have done alone: a rounding of Cape Horn under sail, the sailor's equivalent of scaling Mount Everest. Sailing around the Horn on a square-rigger is something that fewer than 500 living sailors have done, and we, as a team, pulled it off and joined their ranks. It was the creation and development of this highly functioning team that appealed to my background as a management consultant, and is the basis for this book.

The title "Haul Away!" comes from a sailing command used to signal that a group was to pull as hard as possible on a line. The phrase "haul away" is frequently featured in sea shanties sung by a crew, typically when they all had to pull in unison on one of the ship's many lines. The work was backbreaking and dangerous, and required absolute harmony to be done safely and effectively.

A dropped line was a hazard to both crew and the ship. It could cause lost fingers or hands, wrap around an ankle and sweep people overboard, or worse, allow a sail to be caught in the wrong orientation to a storm wind, and shear off a mast, placing the entire vessel at risk. The rhythm of the shanty helped everybody feel the moment when they should grab more line, when they should pull with all their might, and when they should grab a few more inches and get ready to haul again.

On the *Europa*, I noticed that this was one task that we got steadily better at, as we became a more effective team. Part of the challenge was arranging people in the right place, with the right function for each crewmember. As we got deeper into the Southern Ocean, and conditions became more extreme, it wasn't unusual to have 6 or 8 people on a single line. With the wind shrieking in the rigging, the command "Haul away!" would be shouted by the Captain or Mate, and relayed by shouting from person-to-person across the decks until we could hear. There was someone placed at the front of the hauling team, who would repeat the command, "Haul away!" This front-person was at the greatest risk, since they were the one who ultimately had to secure the line back to the pin, at the edge of the ship's sides, a task that routinely mashed fingers if the team behind you didn't keep the proper tension on the line, and let up when asked. Needless to say, this front-person would be first overboard if everybody behind them let go, which struck me as an interesting management image.

Like any team, we were awkward when we started. There were seasoned experts, whose impatience at other's ineptness could barely be concealed, leaving newcomers even more afraid to try. The least able, but most eager to learn, often jumped to the first position on the hauling team, with skinned knuckles and bruised egos the result. Yet there was at least one patient coach on every watch, who knew in the long run they would have to let us make mistakes, and bear more of the load until we learned how to haul away with grace.

By the time we were deep into the Southern Ocean, and nearing Cape Horn, I was impressed how, in the worsening conditions, we were able to function as a smooth team. Regardless of the mix of crew around at any time, we seemed to know how to fall into position, often 6 or 8 people in a row, and haul in a beautiful rhythm, with the odd good-natured foul-up, and move a line against tons of force. Wondering how we got that way was the impetus for this book.

Chapter 1:
The Need for a Quest

It is late summer, and I am enjoying an evening on my small sailboat "Mischief II", moored in downtown Vancouver. Sleeping aboard the boat one night a week has been a favourite tradition of mine for a few years. I am reading a book called "Two Against Cape Horn", as the boat gently bobs and rocks against the marina slip where she is tied up safely. An oil lantern casts a warm glow over the cabin, and if I close my eyes, I can almost imagine that I am sailing offshore, bound for the Southern Ocean, and Cape Horn. I have a small library of books onboard the boat, and the titles betray my fascination with this landmark at the end of the earth: "Godforsaken Sea", "The Blind Horn's Hate", The Last of the Cape Horners", "Once is Enough", "Cape Horn: One Man's Dream, One Woman's Nightmare." After a while, I extinguish the lantern, put my book away, and let the motion of the boat rock me to sleep.

Rob Duncan

In late August 2002, my career was going well. I had been teaching at the British Columbia Institute of Technology for years, following several years of management consulting, including a stint at one of the so-called "Big" firms. Yet something was missing. Although I was engaged in my teaching, I was feeling an emptiness that I attributed to mid-life, since I had recently turned 40. One night it occurred to me that what was missing was Cape Horn, a place I had dreamed about sailing around for much of my life. Like many people with small boats and big dreams, I didn't see how it could be possible. Nonetheless, I was conscious of running out of time, and excuses.

I decided to check the Internet and did a Google search on "Cape Horn." High on the list of hits was a link with a summary that went something like "join the bark Europa for its historic rounding of Cape Horn." I followed the link to www.barkeuropa.com and was struck by a majestic tall ship on the home page. There was a link for the Cape Horn voyage, and clicking on it, I learned that the ship would be sailing the traditional Cape Horner route from San Diego around Cape Horn to the Falklands in a duplication of Richard Henry Dana's return voyage, chronicled in the book "Two Years Before the Mast" published in 1840. They were still looking for deckhand trainees, and were leaving on September 16th, in a few weeks.

Haul Away!

Getting the time off work was the biggest obstacle, and once obtained, everything quickly began to fall into place after that. I was an experienced sailor with my own sailboat for years, so I didn't need much in the way of equipment – just a good set of offshore foul-weather gear befitting the Southern Ocean and Cape Horn, a part of the world with a scary reputation for 100 foot waves, fierce gales, and danger. And there was also the earring.

I needed an earring. More daunting, I needed to get my left earlobe pierced. I had never had anything pierced before, and ironically, it was the ear-piercing that proved to be one of the more challenging aspects of getting ready to go. I decided that the place to get it done was the Hudson's Bay Company, an ancient Canadian institution that gave me warm fuzzies dating from my childhood. I had visions of kind, blue-haired ladies who carefully sterilized their instruments, and who would handle my case with compassion and discretion. Perhaps they even would have known some old Cape Horners from the age of sail. Sadly, on my first foray to the Bay, as the store is known, the ear piercing department was crawling with people – young people. I wasn't about to go in there looking like some pathetic middle-aged man trying to seem young. How would they know that my heroes were long-dead mariners, not rappers?

Rob Duncan

After a few days of casing the place, my moment arrived. I hustled in, and was assured by everybody that it wouldn't hurt. It took a few seconds, after I had chosen the small diamond stud that would serve as a placeholder for the gold hoop I would insert after rounding the Cape. It hurt like hell. I was ready to go.

Cape Horn

Cape Horn lies at the southern tip of North America, where Chile and Argentina meet on their way down toward Antarctica, although Cape Horn itself belongs to Chile. The Cape is said to be the graveyard of some 800 ships and 10,000 sailors. A combination of factors contributes to Cape Horn's dreaded reputation. First, the Southern Ocean's seas whip around this part of the earth unimpeded by land, with the swells reaching towering heights. Winds are likewise unimpeded, and these forces come together at Cape Horn in a situation where the gap between landmasses narrows dramatically, and the sea becomes suddenly quite shallow. The result is a set of conditions that makes Cape Horn the most frightening place on earth to get into trouble in a sailboat. This is also the Horn's allure. There is no higher achievement for a sailor than to have sailed around Cape Horn, and have lived to tell tales of mountainous seas and near-death experiences. In sailing tradition, a Cape Horner is permitted to eat with their feet up on the table in any ship's dining room, is able to spit and urinate into the wind, and is permitted to wear a gold earring in their left ear, signifying their achievement to fellow sailors.

Personal Insights:

1. Anyone who joins a project by choice, or who seeks a new challenge is often responding to a perceived gap between his or her current situation and a possible new situation or way of being. Perhaps we can envision, however hazily, some "new self" that will emerge on the other end of the project or challenge. Maybe we will be more skilled, have more leadership abilities, be more promotable, or unlearn some fears that have been holding us back. This is the quest.

2. One of the keys in this stage of the quest is to allow yourself to feel the gaps that exist for yourself, between where you are and where you would like to be. This sounds easy, but it is one of the toughest parts of a quest. You have to allow yourself to be cranky, disappointed and unhappy, the same parts of ourselves we are encouraged to hide. We need to feel safe to voice our dissatisfaction and to know that it is okay to feel like this. I would not suggest confiding these feelings to your boss, co-workers or anyone with whom you don't have a deeply intimate connection. I would even go easy on partners and good friends: ultimately

they cannot solve the problem for you – it is between you and yourself. You are the person who has to hear how frustrated you are, and your quest only has to make sense to you. Try to go away to a private place – for me it is my boat – and give voice out loud to your frustrations: You wanted to be here, and you are not. You're getting older, and less able to take the risks you hoped you would, and so on. Let it all out. It may feel lousy at first, but one of the major hurdles to achieving what you want will have been removed – because now it is out there. You will find that you can't get the genie back in the bottle once you have given voice to it.

Teambuilding Lessons:

1. Gap analysis is the basis for every project or team effort. Be frank in where you are and where you would like to end up. By defining the gap clearly and honestly, you will make sure that you undertake the right project for the proper reasons.

2. Every project begins with research. It is critical to do enough homework to be certain that you are creating the right project, for the right reasons, and involving the right people.

3. It is useful at the outset of a new project to unfreeze some of your precepts about the nature and structure of the project and the team that will execute it. In my case, I had a desire to round Cape Horn at some point in my life, and sooner rather than later. By doing some research, I found that there was a way to get around the Horn that was quite different that what I had envisioned: A big tall ship instead of a small sailboat; leaving from San Diego, instead of home.

Personal Development Worksheet #1:

1. What are the gaps in my life?

2. If I had no excuses (eg. no time, lack of money, responsibilities), what could I do to address one of these gaps?

3. If I successfully addressed this one gap in my life, what would be different about me? About my life?

4. "Plan B": What might be another way to close this gap in my life?

5. What one thing will I accomplish this coming week to start my quest in motion?

6. Who can support my goals at this stage?

Chapter 2:
Casting Off

I have just been shown to my "rack", one of six bunks in Cabin 12, where I will sleep for the next 75 days. The heat down below is oppressive, as the hot San Diego sun has been beating down on the ship for days. There is one small porthole that can be opened to let in some natural light through the thick glass, but no fresh air can come in. My rack lies parallel to the side of the ship, which I know from small boats is the best orientation when things get tilted out there. I wonder who my cabin mates will be? I crawl into my new home to check it out. It is around 2 feet wide and six and a half feet long – kind of like me. I slide in and lie back. There is about a foot and a half of space above my head where the upper bank is. There are a couple of small wooden shelves, and a curtain for privacy. A small fan is attached to the wall around 4 feet away, but it isn't working right now. I feel a rising sense of panic.

Haul Away!

I flew out of Vancouver to San Diego on September 12th, one year and a day after the 9/11 tragedy, and airport security was extremely tight. It didn't help that I had a couple of big duffle bags full of weird stuff, like goggles, knives and a GPS. I decided to be honest: "Why are you coming to the US today?" "I'm joining a tall ship in San Diego and we are going to sail around Cape Horn." "And when are you leaving the States"? "In a few days." Long pause. "Have a good trip." I was handed back my documents. The rest of the flights were smooth, and I landed in San Diego. My cab went right by the *Europa* on the way to the hotel, and I felt a huge thrill of excitement. I was determined not to announce myself to the ship until the last minute, because I wanted a few days to get my head around the idea that this voyage was really going to happen.

I checked into my hotel, and crashed for a while in front of the TV, the air conditioning giving some relief from the nauseating heat. "In a few weeks, you are going to be at the equator, with no relief whatsoever", I thought to myself. "If you go", I added. Self-doubt was beginning to double me over. After a pizza and a couple of beers, and another review of the ship's literature, I began to feel better, but the self-doubt that I couldn't last 75 days on a boat with no escape kept gnawing at me.

I wandered around San Diego for the next 2 days, distracting myself at the zoo and with numerous trips up and down the trolley lines. I found a nice café I liked, and spent many hours there keeping my journals and talking by phone to my wife, who by this time was in Toronto starting her Master's degree, her own voyage.

Departure day came, and I checked out of the hotel, humped my bags into a cab and descended the big hill to the pier. I walked the gangplank, scooting past the "mere tourists". Already I felt special, and a part of the vessel. I introduced myself to an exceptionally tall guy named Seth, the First Mate, who would later end up being my watch leader. Next, I was drawn to a silver-haired gentleman who I took to be Geoff, the Englishman I had read about in a news story on the Internet. Geoff was agreeably stamping "passports" for visitors to the ship. The passports were a popular feature of the tall ships festival. People could visit each ship, and receive a stamp unique to the ship in a booklet. I was eager to be a contributing member from the get-go, so I offered to spell Geoff and spent the next hour or so stamping these passports. It felt good. People reflected their envy of my voyage, and it pumped me up.

Later though, I felt the awkward silence of all the crew, some Dutch, some American, some British and a scattering of others like me, the lone Canadian. There were a bunch of folks who had been on the boat for months, and several who were leaving. I knew it wasn't our voyage yet, and wouldn't be until we cast off for good the next day.

Haul Away!

The *Europa* in San Diego

Sleep was impossible that first night. The heat was unbearable – and I had slept on trains through India in the hot season; I wasn't that inflexible. The next day, rumors of us not leaving began to filter down in various languages and versions. There was a tropical depression forming off the coast, or something was broken, or something hadn't arrived, or some person hadn't arrived yet. It went on and on, and the jump-ship urge came over me. If I can't sleep, and the heat gets worse and worse, how can I survive for two and a half months? I started to concoct a secret plan whereby I could jump off the boat, snake my way down through South American café society to somewhere near Cape Horn, and then jump on one of those "quickie" boat tours that whip you around the Horn in a couple of days, then hand you your earring and certificate. After all, who would be the wiser back home? My brain was getting feverish.

We didn't leave that day, or the next. The third day, I sat down with my new friend Geoff and asked: "I'm worried that I can't do this. I'm not sleeping. I'm thinking about jumping ship." He looked shocked, and just then Tracy called my cell phone. "I'm just talking with Geoff, I'm thinking of jumping ship and joining the ship on Easter Island next month." "Don't be crazy. Go, you'll have a great time. And you would really regret it forever if you bailed out now. You can do this."

"Make voyages. Attempt them. There is nothing else."

Tennessee Williams

After the call, Geoff verbalized what had been plain on his face: "Don't be silly. You would always wonder if you did the right thing, for the rest of your life." I calmed down, and was saved by the ship's horn sounding. "Prepare to cast off" came the order from the Captain, Klaas Gaastra. Finally, an end to indecision. It felt great to pull away from land and see Dana Point recede off into the distance as the sun set.

Haul Away!

Leaving land

Man Overboard!

On the *Europa*, we practiced man overboard and fire drills. This was done early in the voyage to determine where we were strong and where we needed more practice. In its simplest form, a man overboard drill involves throwing a floating buoy overboard and shouting, "Man overboard!" There are roles and responsibilities that each person has during a man overboard situation, and it is critical to saving a life that each task happen when it should. There is a spotter, ideally the first person to see the person fall overboard, whose job it is to alert everybody that a sailor is overboard, and then to keep the overboard sailor in his or her eyesight at all times, pointing to them in the water so that others can pick up the sighting. The more people that know where the person is in the water, the more likely the person can be rescued. Someone needs to get a flotation device with a heaving line over to the person in the water, the person steering the ship must know what to do, and so forth. A similar drill is practiced for fire situations. The fire drills ended up serving us well when we had a real fire in the middle of the night thousands of miles offshore. Some rags had caught fire dangerously close to where the paints and solvents were stored, but we managed to handle the situation safely thanks to practice.

In a team or project setting, it also makes sense to have drills in anticipation of things going wrong. These don't have to be high stress situations like on a ship, but why not ask questions like: "How would and should we react as a team if...." If our deadline was shortened by 2 weeks, if our budget was reduced by 15%, if our competition rushes their product to market next week, and so on. A quick 5-minute discussion is all that is needed. The purpose of the drills is to focus the team's attention on possible things that could go wrong, and to build confidence in the team's ability to adapt to and cope with situations. Most importantly, these drills help build an "early warning" instinct in the team because they focus part of the team's attention on the signals to watch for before negative disruption happens. Anybody on the team should be able to call a drill, not just the team leader.

Personal Insights:

1. Fear and indecision are normal anytime you undertake a new challenge or quest. Similar to the way we let the genie out of the bottle and gave voice to our dissatisfactions and frustrations, we also need to feel free to accept that feeling ambivalent and fearful is part of the course that will lead us out the other end of our quest. It is perfectly normal and healthy to want to swim back to shore. These are ancient instincts that have kept us alive through the centuries.

> ***"Remember: sooner or later, we've all got to face it."***
>
> Captain Christopher Sheldon, from the movie "White Squall"

2. These feelings of fear and indecision are the worst part of any new undertaking, because they precede the moment of commitment, the moment when the shore becomes out of reach, the moment when you are on board for the voyage whether you like it or not. It is important not to rush through this fear and indecision phase, but clearly you have to get past it. If you find yourself putting off decisions and quests over and over again, you may be falling into a pattern of failing to gain the necessary traction to make your vision for yourself in the future become reality. This is where reaching out to others can help.

3. How many times have we summoned our courage and admitted to some seemingly invincible friend or colleague that we felt nervous at the outset of some endeavor only to have them say, "Wow, you were nervous? I thought I was the only one!" The fact is that anyone who is not nervous at the outset of a new challenge is probably not equipped to succeed at it. They may lack the necessary honesty to be able to gauge

their abilities, or they may only choose easy projects that involve no growth. So now that we know that we are all in the same boat – let's talk about it. Reaching out to others during these moments is critical to breaking through the anxiety and getting truly committed.

4. Finally: don't back out. Commit to your dreams. Regret is the biggest enemy you will face, as you get older.

"Twenty years from now you will be more disappointed by the things that you didn't do than by the ones you did do. So throw off the bowlines. Sail away from the safe harbour. Catch the trade winds in your sails. Explore. Dream. Discover."

Mark Twain

Teambuilding Lessons:

1. All team members new to a project are going to feel some anxiety at its outset. Some of their fears may relate to failing, to not being up to the task at hand, or to not blending in socially. It is important for the manager to encourage the voicing of these fears in order to underscore that everyone may be dealing with these personal insecurities. Similarly, peer-to-peer sharing of anxieties can

be very helpful in dissipating these fears and encouraging early bonding of the team.

2. The above situation is even more acute when people on a team can opt out of participating. This was my case in the Cape Horn trip, while still in San Diego. Realistically, I had all the weeks before meeting the ship up to, say, 50 feet offshore to back out and swim back to land! There is no question that the worst part of the voyage for me was during these weeks leading up to commitment. Despite all the real dangers that were to come, the indecision of whether to follow-through and commit or not was the most agonizing phase. This is no different on any team effort where people have not yet committed to the task at hand. The manager can help by airing this fact and assuring team members that, as tough as the project is to get at times, there will be nothing as bad as the time prior to locking-in and joining the group effort.

Personal Development Worksheet #2

1. What is it about my personal challenge or quest that I fear?

2. What is it about the possibility of failing that that makes me afraid?

3. Do I fear success on some level? Why?

4. Assuming my greatest fears about my quest come true, what would happen to me?

5. Ignoring the worst and best case scenarios, what is realistically probably going to happen if I pursue my quest?

6. Which 3 people I am going to share my quest vision with in the coming week?

Chapter 3:
Out of Sight of Land

Yikes! The waves are getting bigger, and I still haven't really slept well. It is murderously hot, and we are gunning both engines in order to try to get over top of a tropical depression that is tearing up the coast of Mexico toward us, wreaking havoc as it goes. To a sailor, there are few things less satisfying than motoring with the sails furled away, against the natural flow of the waves. I am surprised how much rolling a boat this size does while motoring. I have also been struggling to climb the rigging, a critical skill for a tall ship sailor, who needs to go aloft to set and strike sails. The experienced sailors can scramble up to the top of the masts, almost 100 feet in the air, and make it look easy. For me, more at home with a tub of ice cream than a climbing wall, it is proving to be a defeating challenge. There is a nasty piece of hardware called the futtocks shroud, around 30 feet up that requires you to lean backwards and try to propel yourself both upwards and outwards over the ocean at the same time – kind of like walking on the ceiling. You need to get beyond this spot to keep climbing. I am good at scrambling up the first 30 feet, but the futtocks shroud has me stymied. If I am this uncomfortable at this point of the voyage, how will I last another 65 days in worsening conditions? Just how bad will things get?

Europa with her studding-sails set

A few days later, having eluded the tropical depression, we were finally able to point down south a bit, and get the sails up, 24 of them at one point. The difference in my mood compared to the first few days is striking. I felt much more at home both on the ship and with the ocean.

What changed? First, as the seas were building, I tried to focus on the reactions of the more experienced offshore sailors, who seemed more bored than afraid. When I came up on deck after an off-watch shift – to see waves bigger that I had ever personally seen, I fell into the habit of looking around at the others, and forcing my own gut reactions back down into a context that would make sense to people who could be more relaxed about the situation than I could. These were not lunatics, just experienced deep-water sailors, and their reactions – or lack thereof – to the situation, were the ones that made sense.

I can now see that what I was feeling was a very real lack of experience and skills as a sailor. I had single-handed my own little boat around home waters in BC, and was quite comfortable doing that. But it was a far cry from being offshore in 10-foot seas, on a complex vessel with some 200 lines that controlled some 24 sails and their various yards. It was only normal that I would be scared of not knowing what I was doing – I didn't!

Colleagues came to the rescue again. During this time, we had been divided into 2 watches, port watch and starboard watch, an old tradition from the age of sail. This meant that the crew of 24 people was now split into 2 teams of 12 people each. This accomplished a couple of things. It meant that half of us could sleep while the other half worked the ship. It also meant that there was a smaller subculture that each of us

Haul Away!

could identify with. Finally, it opened the door to a new phenomenon: good-natured but persistent competition.

I was a member of the "port" watch, port being an arbitrary name that refers to the left-hand side of the ship, starboard being the right-hand side. In reality, these names for the 2 watches had nothing to do with right or left. What was important was the port watch was my tribe – these were my people. Not that there was anything wrong with the starboard watch – I had got to know them as the voyage began – I just didn't want to be one of them. This splitting into two teams formed two different subcultures that were beginning to bond. We were led by Seth, who was the First Mate and second-in-command to the Captain of the ship. The Captain led the other watch.

Belonging to a smaller subgroup that was part of the larger team gave me a home for my friendships and fears. I was in the same watch as Geoff, my first friend on the voyage, who had inspired me to stay on board in the beginning. From there, other relationships were free to grow. Geoff, another sailor named Colin and I soon formed an ad hoc team that specialized in woodwork when we weren't actually sailing the ship. We sat together and scraped old varnish off all kinds of wooden blocks and other apparatus that had been taken down from the rigging – part of the never-ending maintenance of a traditional old ship. Hour after hour saw us sitting together, shooting the breeze, and laboriously scraping every millimeter of old varnish off the wooden pieces, then sanding them down to a smooth finish, and eventually re-varnishing them with 8 or 9 coats of new varnish. The beauty of this work was that you could always have something to occupy yourself with when the boat was sailing smoothly – a small portable task that you could set aside when the call-up came to set or strike sails, or it was your turn to take the helm for an hour. As I think back to it, these wood-scraping tasks served a very specific role in mitigating and managing my fears of the unknown.

First, the wood-scraping allowed each of us to become an expert in some small part of the ship's operation, early on in the voyage. It wasn't long before exasperated members of the other watch would come by during watch transitions and say: "I've been trying to get this block back in the rigging for days, and can't find the time. I hear you guys are the best." This was a confidence booster that led to an appetite for greater expertise.

Second, the rituals and routines of our little team of woodworking experts provided a regular chance for banter. I could ask fellow sailors whether they thought the previous night's squall – in which we had blown out a couple sails amid much shouting – was worth being concerned about, and could hear: "Nah, we blew out sails all the time on my trip through the Bay of Biscay last year, and that was in Force 10 conditions. If you're not blowing out old sails like these, you probably aren't pushing hard enough. Just wait until…" This gave me an ongoing context for my reactions to new experiences. Just because I had never blown out a sail in my own little sailboat didn't mean I had to be overly afraid of doing so out here in the deep ocean. I vowed to stay close to the people who were coping easily with new experiences; they counterbalanced that side of myself that I wasn't happy with; they had what I needed.

Last, the routine of having a small task to accomplish formed a bridge between crises. There would always be hectic moments of frantic activity, when a crisis was happening, and the ship and sails needed urgent tending, but somewhere in the recesses of my mind, there was that place of routine and friendly banter to get back to. It was surprisingly comforting to know that some niggling task was waiting for me once things calmed down.

Wearing Ship

There is a maneuver on a tall ship that is similar to a gybe on a smaller sailboat. The rear of the ship is brought through the wind, and then the sails are reset on a new course. On a ship with some 24 sails, this is not a simple task. The vessel has to be steered carefully through a set of course changes while the captain directs the furling, setting and bracing of sails and yards. This is accomplished by careful communication between the captain and the helm, the person steering the ship's wheel. The captain directs the setting of the sails, and relays course changes to the helm, who must respond in a measured but timely fashion to bring the ship around so that the next set of adjustments can be made to the sails. "What is your course?" "One-forty". "Okay, come up to one-fifty" "Aye-aye, one-fifty…there's one-fifty." And so it continues until the ship is brought around safely onto its new course. A captain and helm working together for the first time is not usually very elegant, but if you put an experienced helm and experienced captain together, the maneuvering is very sweet. The helm anticipates the captain's next command, and the captain can be confident that the next adjustment is probably already underway just as the captain is about to call for it. In all teams, this highlights the value of synergy between people who know what others require and get in the habit of working together in ways that make for smooth team functioning. At all levels, this involves sharing what everybody on the team does and how they do it. The purpose is not to enable everyone to do each function, but rather to gain an understanding of the needs and constraints that each person encounters in trying to make a contribution to the team's goals. This involves a measure of openness that needs to be encouraged by the team's leaders.

Personal Insights:

1. Turning new corners in a project or quest is always fraught with uncertainty and some degree of fear. Seek out others on or outside the team and allow your reactions to situations to be dictated as much as possible by theirs. This isn't to suggest that you should run like a herd of lemmings over a cliff if your gut says not to, but rather that you should look to the people who seem confident in a crisis or in a particular new territory, and ask yourself why that is so. Ask them as well. The alternative – which many of us have done – is to seek out people with the same fears and insecurities as ourselves, and hunker down around a figurative water cooler, and collectively convince ourselves that, indeed, the project is off the rails and can't possibly succeed.

2. Getting part-way there is still an achievement: accept partial victories. I wanted to climb to the very top of the rigging, over 100 feet in the air. At 6'2" and a not-very-athletic 200-plus pounds, nature and gravity had other designs for me. Quite afraid of heights, I broke the goal into steps, the first being getting over the first hurdle, the nasty futtocks shroud, some 30 feet up. Once that was bested, I went a little higher. Each time, I came back down feeling a mixture of elation and disappointment in myself. Eventually, on a later tall ship voyage, I managed to get 80 feet or so up into the rig, but still, the top eluded me, and I certainly was never comfortable up there. After beating up on myself for not being better able to climb, I realized that I should be content with the tasks I was good at and comfortable with, like helming, and see the challenges like climbing as something I could continue to work on over the years. I can now see each progression upwards into the rig as a big personal success for me, rather than as an ongoing failure. The next time I am on board *Europa* or another tall ship, I know that I will be able to scamper over the futtocks shroud that once kept me down on deck, and I will progress up a little further each trip.

Haul Away!

3. Show up a few minutes early. A small amount of consideration pays huge dividends in team morale. Showing up a few minutes early when you are due to relieve somebody is one of the most powerful morale boosters I have seen on a ship. When you are on a watch system, everybody on the watch takes a turn doing each job on the ship, often for a half-hour or hour at a time. The jobs vary, from being lookout on the bow, to steering the boat. The tradition is that once you have done your "trick", or stretch of work, you can rest for a while in the deckhouse to warm up, cool down, get a coffee, or whatever you feel like doing until your next trick comes up. I made it a habit to show up a few minutes early whenever I was due to replace someone. The exchange usually went like this:

"I'm here to relieve you. I'm a few minutes early, and I don't mean to rush you, but if you've had enough I am happy to take over."

I never saw a negative reaction. There were times, such as a peaceful night on bow watch when the person you were to relieve was enjoying looking at the stars and could stay there forever, that the offer was politely declined. But there were also hideous times on the helm in a hail squall where the chance to exit a bit early toward a hot cup of coffee was hugely appreciated. It meant I had a few minutes less in the deckhouse for myself, but the habit quickly spread, and it wasn't long before I was also getting relieved a few minutes early, so it balanced out. The payback in morale was huge. Everybody felt like they were doing a bit extra and pitching in a little bit more, and the person being relieved never had the "have they forgotten me out here?" feeling, which is a lousy feeling in a hail squall.

In organizations, this can be a consciously engrained habit of taking a little off the next person's task list. It can be as simple as walking into a situation and seeing something you could do, right then and there, that somebody else would have to do eventually. I may be the CEO, but is there any reason I can't lead the effort to clean up the paper plates and juice cans after the meeting? It's contagious, can be started by any team member at any level, and spreads through a team quickly. One of my favourite moments on watch was when someone came to relieve me early, using my same "I'm a few minutes early" line.

Haul Away!

Teambuilding Lessons:

1. Give thought to pairing novices with experienced people in small sub-projects, or mini-teams. Similarly, try to group the chronic naysayer with the insufferable optimist, and so forth. It won't be the smoothest project you ever ran, but the likelihood of success is far greater by not allowing synergistically negative groups to form.

2. Likewise, consider splitting the project team into 2 smaller groups that have overlapping responsibilities, similar to a port and a starboard watch. Let the competitive spirit that emerges between these 2 groups flourish unless it becomes destructive to the overall end goal of the project. Let each team foster their own identities and imagery; let them name themselves.

3. Everyone should own a small part of the overall routine of the project. Like scraping a particular block, that can be set aside in a crisis, and returned to later, a small part of the routine that is uniquely owned by each team member can be an important buffer to manage through the ups and downs of a project.

4. Re-frame failures into partial successes when appropriate. Everyone wants each attempt at a goal to be a smashing success, but realistically they rarely are. If we see these outings as failures, then negative thinking will spiral and grow. If we made progress, and got a little further ahead, that is a success, not a failure. We will regroup and get even further later, but let's recognize that we did achieve something.

5. Create and support a learning culture. Everybody has something to contribute.

On the ship, we started a tradition of holding seminars at 3pm, just after the full crew meeting, while both watches were still awake. Everyone was encouraged to contribute a topic and lead a seminar, and these ranged from Polynesian canoeing traditions, to lunar navigation, to Internet marketing. The point was not so much the session content, but rather that we were all expected to be part of a teaching and learning culture. Attendance was optional, and many people on the retiring watch were too tired to attend, but a small crowd of crewmates would be there for each session (if nothing else, it was a break from more mundane tasks.) The seminars also helped build an understanding of each other's lives off the ship, and the many talents everyone had to share. In a team setting, this is an excellent way of setting a cultural expectation that everyone must share their knowledge, and that team members each have something unique to contribute: the most junior team member may be a world-class snowboarder, and the CEO may write mystery novels.

Personal Development Worksheet #3

1. What is one thing that I am good at? How can I make that ability my signature or calling card on the team?

2. Who on my team always seems a little more together and composed in new situations than the rest of us? How can I spend more time with them?

3. Who can I help develop or mentor, so that they are more comfortable with new tasks on the team?

4. What will I say to myself when I feel my old fears creeping up on me?

5. What is one personal ritual that I will use to mark milestones on my quest?

Chapter 4:
Steady as she Goes

We have been offshore for a month now, and are nearing the equator. We are all better sailors, and have been through most situations that we expected to see – at least until we get down into the Roaring Forties and Furious Fifties that lead around Cape Horn. We occasionally have a new enemy: routine and boredom.

> **"We are making miles each day, but since we are going more south than west, we are not getting any closer to our destination."**
>
> Captain Klaas Gaastra

Our "woodworking team" has expanded our repertoire to include other areas of expertise, including rust busting, metal painting, rope and wire splicing and sail stitching. These maintenance skills are in addition to the skills of sailing the ship itself: helming, bracing the yards, setting and striking sails, going aloft to furl or unfurl the sails.

Sails have been blown out, stitched, and blown out again. Crises are handled with aplomb, and the port watch is becoming a tighter team. But there is a new phenomenon: familiarity is breeding contempt. That, and it is getting bloody hot as we draw closer to the equator. My nightmare scenario of a few weeks ago (we will be overwhelmed by terrible sea conditions and die) has been replaced by a new one: what if I can't stand these people for another month and a half without going crazy?

There is an ancient rite of passage that is important to most sailors who aspire to become deep-water veterans: that of becoming a "shellback." A shellback is a sailor who has crossed the equator under sail, thus graduating from the rank of "pollywog." This rite of passage has been remarkably stable through the ages, in that it is marked with a sort of hazing in which the existing shellbacks sit in judgement of those who wish to reach shellback status, but have yet to cross the equator. The process is that of a court tribunal, in which King Neptune (often played by the captain) and his henchmen humiliate the pollywogs in a mock trial, complete with a detailing of past "crimes", and punishments to be meted out. Rotten food, blindfolds, razors and buckets of vile substances form a part of the ritual – you get the general idea. The beauty of the ceremony is that once you have been through it and have become a shellback yourself, you can then be part of the judging tribunal the next time. You never have to go through it twice.

As we drew closer to the equator, there began to be not-so-secret meetings of the shellbacks, which we were forbidden to intrude upon. The deckhouse would reverberate with sinister laughter these evenings, as we clicked along down the latitudes toward the equator: 5 degrees, 4 degrees, 3 degrees – about a degree every day. We started to wake up with scrawling on our cabin doors, like "Hair today, gone tomorrow," an allusion to the head-shaving that was a famous part of the traditional shellback ritual. A day or so before we crossed 00:00.00 degrees, the latitude of the equator, a large, person-sized catapult was wordlessly erected on the deck, facing out toward the ocean.

For a bunch of grown-ups, I had to admit we were all pretty nervous. But this was an essential part of the fun. It revived our flagging spirits, and created a new positive schism in the crew: us versus them, pollywogs versus shellbacks. It was exactly what we had needed. The day of the crossing itself was as bad and as exciting as we had feared. About 20 of us were herded into the hottest cabin in the bowels of the ship, and were left to swelter there for over an hour, as the scent of days-old chicken guts and fish pieces was piped into the cabin by King Neptune's henchmen. It was hellish. Relief, such as it was, came in the form of being blindfolded, and led, one-by-one up through the ship to the deck, where Neptune and his cronies awaited. Once there, we were bathed in a disgusting mess of rotten beans, old beer, spit, and the sound of an electric razor buzzed in our ears. Our crimes were recited: "You are charged with being too nice all the time. Your sentence is to insult so-and-so, who is next up, using this loudhailer, for a period of not less than 5 minutes." After these and other indignities, we were tattooed with black tar and pronounced shellbacks. We were elated. We got to wash up, and the instigators nobly took on the job of washing up all the messes. A big party ensued on the main deck, and the entire crew – shellbacks all – rocked the night away.

The crew of both watches celebrates crossing the Equator

Haul Away!

It was great to bond as one big team again, port and starboard watch all awake at the same time, reconnecting. Changes were to come soon. The next day, the Captain announced a number of substantial trades: "So-and-so, over to port watch; you, over to starboard watch..." It was like 2 competing sports teams doing a "heart transplant:" the guts of both our teams were ripped out and swapped. It was nerve-wracking. Strong personalities we had eyed from afar were now on our watch, while the heart and soul of our team was gone. It took a long time for us all to get over it, but one thing is for certain: we all tried harder to impress, especially the newcomers, who knew that sentiment was working against them.

The "2 O'Clockie"

We had a shipboard tradition, devised by the Captain, called the "2 O'Clockie". This was a meeting led by the Captain in which each crew member was called upon individually to offer up any concerns, questions, kudos, irritations, or anything else on their minds. These meetings happened everyday, at 2pm ship's time. Even in the roughest weather, the meetings took place, in some form, even if we were hanging from the lifelines as water rushed over the decks. The Captain led off the meeting by telling us how far we had sailed in the last 24 hours, the weather trends, some general comments on what was going well or badly, as well as sharing the basics of any strategic issues he was weighing at his level. Then he started with a crewmember, picked at random, and called each person by name. We were all given the chance to express anything on our minds, such as a question or concern. Most of us just smiled and said we were okay with everything. Occasionally, a concern was offered: "Would people please clean their own skid marks off the toilet bowl up forward. That is what the brush is for!" The Captain would weigh in with a word or support, or just acknowledge that the person had been heard. A lot of the time, people who had something to say, didn't. Or maybe they waited a day or two to see if anyone else would bring the issue up, and then they would speak up. If people tried to talk to the Captain alone, he would say: "That's a perfect thing to bring up at the next 2 O'Clockie, You see, you did have something to say after all."

The teambuilding lesson here is that the leader or group facilitator should regularly have a time when all team members can voice concerns. And this meeting must be a regular feature with a set schedule, even if it is done electronically or in some other format than face-to-face. This tactic fails when team members – the leader included – start feeling that everything is going "okay" and they don't need these regular check-in meetings. Nobody will suggest the meetings start again when things go off the rails, and this is how things fester. Keep it regular, keep it brief, and keep in happening both in good and bad times. Be prepared to hear what you don't want to hear. As a team member, be prepared to speak up. If you don't, not only will you personally suffer in silence, but also the team will be less effective as a whole. Remember that leadership is not just the job of one person, but of everybody on the team. Sometimes leadership is as simple as "cleaning up your own skid marks." Or calling the team on it when it isn't being done.

Personal Insights:

1. Routine can end up being as much of an enemy as fear. Contriving ways to shake things up can help you stay focused

and engaged. Have a celebration, and mark a successful crossing. Then get ready for a curve ball.

2. There is a fine line between being comfortable and becoming complacent. It is a good idea to anticipate that a surprise is usually just around the corner, and be ready to roll with it.

3. Positive stress is highly bonding for a team. The tension created by the build-up to our "shellback ceremony" was very uplifting and energizing. By having a common threat to deal with, the "pollywogs" became a very tightly-knit team.

Teambuilding Lessons:

1. Be mindful of the need for celebrations of milestones. Not so many that every day ends in a party, but something that everyone can see coming for some time, and which builds in importance in the minds of each team member.

2. Take the pulse of the team regularly, whether or not you think the feedback is going to be positive. The ship's "2 O'Clockie" meetings were always held, rain or shine, and everyone knew that they could voice any concerns or

aggravations they had. The captain was also able to share any new information with everybody, and seek advice and input. This tradition did a lot to enhance teambuilding and open communication on board the ship.

3. When comfort becomes counterproductive, consider a shake-up. Two effective methods of doing this are a celebration of a rite of passage related to a major project milestone or a personnel change. In our case, the ship's captain used both effectively. The build-up to the equator-crossing ceremony was extremely effective at getting us productively riled-up, and shaking us out of comfort zone. Also, by swapping some strong personalities between the starboard and the port watches, some calcified relationships were broken up, and new, productive tensions were created.

Personal Development Worksheet #4

1. What am I bored or complacent with in my regular routines?

2. What one thing will I do in the coming week to shake up my routine?

3. At what point on my quest will I become a "shellback"?

4. How will I mark this rite of passage?

5. What symbol or ritual will I use to permanently mark my transition from "pollywog" to "shellback"?

Chapter 5:
First Landfall

I am woken up for my 4am shift with the words "You can see Easter Island!" I am scheduled to be on bow-watch for the first hour, so I hustle up to the main deck and onto the raised bow portion of the ship. Sure enough, in the twilight I can see 2 shapes on the horizon, which look to me like a giant turtle and a sailing sloop. As I grow accustomed to the light, a big island to the left of these shapes begins to fill in. As the morning progresses and dawn continues, we start to smell land, which we haven't done for over 35 days. It is a mixture of smells, some like spice, some like tobacco, and something human and indistinct, maybe a bit dirty. If apprehension has a smell, it would be like this last essence. The fascinating array of scents is destroyed by a crewmember from the other watch who had doused himself in aftershave in anticipation of landing, overwhelming all of the fragrances wafting over the sea. I am reminded at that moment that we have been in too-close quarters for a long time, and if nothing else, that Easter Island should provide a chance for some solitary respite.

We had one stop in our voyage, roughly the halfway point between our starting point of San Diego, and our ending landfall of the Falkland Islands. This was Easter Island. We had been at sea for a long time, the reconstituted port and starboard watches were beginning to gel into effective teams, and we approached land with mixed feelings.

The mysterious stone statues of Easter Island

For one thing, we would be taking on a few new crewmembers – people who wanted to sail around Cape Horn, but who hadn't been able to join the voyage earlier. We viewed them with some suspicion: why should they be able to join now when they hadn't sweated through the last month and a half? Heck, they weren't even shellback, yet we wouldn't even have the satisfaction of putting them through the initiation since we wouldn't cross the equator again as a team. What if they were disruptive, incapable of performing, or downright dangerous? Certainly they weren't part of our well-established team. Fear and loathing hissed along the gossip lines on night watch.

Land itself was a source of ambivalence. For a month and a half, we had found a special peace with the ocean, wind and stars. We had no jobs other than the ones on the ship, and our cares such as bills piling up and so forth were literally thousands of miles away. Easter Island, with its pay telephones and Internet cafés would catapult us back into that other world. We would be at once aware of all that might be going off the rails back home, but at the same time, unable to do much about it. Certainly it would be good to communicate with loved ones, but unsettling as well, since it would underline the isolation of our situation. A few of us wanted to see Easter Island itself, and the great stone head statues, but most of us would have felt better sailing on past.

What was different about these anxieties was that we now felt comfortable enough with each other to voice them, and to help each other calm down a bit about them. As before, I tried to stick like glue to those who weren't troubled, but nevertheless, spent a lot of time worrying with others around the figurative water cooler.

We were getting close to setting the anchor, and the Captain called muster for both watches. Then, we learned that we would be able to be put ashore in groups of around 6 at a time, but in order to keep to schedule, we would only be able to stay for 6 hours. We dropped the hook, and the first boatload went ashore, with me among them. This first boat ferried the new crewmembers back to the ship after dropping us off, but we were all content to let them move onboard by themselves, saving meeting them for later. Six hours was preciously little time to accomplish so many things: catching up with home, getting some solitude, doing some shopping and sightseeing. Given how ambivalent we were about being on land, perhaps it was a mercifully short time. First up for me was solitude. I wandered away from our little shore party at the earliest opportunity and didn't look back. I found a community centre craft market right up the hill from where we landed, and had a great time looking around at all the crafts, enjoying doing something different for a change. I found the Chileans very friendly and helpful with my rusty Spanish. After buying some gifts, I just sat outside and wrote in my journal for an hour. I knew I should be getting out and seeing the famous head sculptures and all the mysteries of Easter Island, but that really wasn't my trip. I was going around Cape Horn, and anything else on the way was just a distraction. After a while, a couple of crewmates I liked happened by and said they were going to rent a car to do some sightseeing, and asked if I wanted to join them. Against my instincts for solitude, I agreed. I would end up regretting this.

Haul Away!

As we headed off in the car, we drove past another crewmate whom I had been hoping to get away from for a few hours. My car-mates, who were from the other watch and not well acquainted with this person, felt that more was merrier, and invited him along. What had started as a comfortable day of sightseeing had already degenerated into a cramped and tense day, with our added crewmate having a series of the same temper tantrums that I had been eager to escape from. I resolved to trust my instincts in the future.

After seeing the sights, and managing to claw a half-hour more of solitude at one of the parks we visited, we went back into town, and I found the Internet cafe. I spent an hour there, finding out what was happening in my life back home, and fixed what I could with a note or two. Nothing major required my attention. Enough was enough. I logged off, paid, bought a handful of chocolate bars, and headed down to the dock. I'd had enough of land and its annoyances. Bring on Cape Horn!

Rob Duncan

Seeing your own Flaws First

We are often thrown into team situations with people who rub us the wrong way. As you look back on your life though, hasn't it often been the case that the people who give you an immediate negative impression sometimes become good friends? On a ship, there is almost always someone who stands out as being careless, or unclean, or mean or any number of other character flaws. It is easy to take a self-centered approach to these people and assume they have been sent there specifically to annoy you. On a sailing ship, though, there is no escape. No walking away from the office, and saying "What a jerk." You may well have the bunk above or below the person annoying you, and they are going to be around 24 hours a day. People who do well on long sailing passages learn one lesson very quickly: keep a long fuse, and be slow to judge others. You can't help forming impressions, but the person you are most irritated by may end up being the person whose hand reaches out to you as you are being swept off deck by a rogue wave. A useful technique is to stop yourself when you are thinking something bad about a team mate, and ask: what would it likely be about *me* that drives this other person crazy? Might they see me as unfriendly? Insecure? Sloppy? If I am honest, I find it is often *my own* qualities reflected in other people that bug me the most. Giving the other person a break

Haul Away!

in this way always provokes a smile in me, and by that point, there is usually a rope to be hauled on or some other real work to be done.

Personal Insights:

1. Trust your instincts, especially where ambivalence is concerned. Check these against more experienced people to give them context, and to distinguish them from self-defeating behaviors. I knew I needed solitude above all else on Easter Island, but didn't follow-through on my gut. I regretted that for some time, as I wasn't able to return to the vessel as recharged as I could have.

2. Solitude is your friend. When you know you need it, take it. This is much better than allowing yourself to be worn down by stress and become a frazzled and grating team member. Ultimately you will be less productive and are less likely to be a positive contributor to the team and its outcome – an outcome that you once bought into as a personal quest. Take your solitary time, and – as in Chapter 1 – go down to your own personal boat (or bathtub) and reflect on where you are, where you hoped to be, and the current state of the gap between the two. The end result of this

time-taking will be a renewed sense of accomplishment, and a freshened perspective on what you are doing and why.

3. When you want to be alone, tell people what you need and you'll usually get it. There are moments on a long voyage with a full crew when you just want 5 minutes to be alone. Unfortunately this desire usually expresses itself as free-floating hostility that leaves everybody edgy, and more often than not, they crowd you even more trying to find out what's wrong, which just feeds your bad mood. Somewhere after my 10,000th ocean mile, I finally learned that it is easier to just say: "Hey man, I really like chatting with you, but I need a few minutes alone to think about stuff." Say it with a smile, however forced. It works well and it works fast – right when you need it. It leaves everybody feeling better, and takes the guesswork out of being around you. Generally people are happy to give you what you want, and happy to see you get it. But you need to let them know what it is you need.

4. Take time to recognize how you have changed, developed and improved. By Easter Island, I was a much more capable sailor and crewmember. My

skills and experience had multiplied over the course of the voyage to that point. Likewise, it is essential that you also take a moment to pat yourself on the back and appreciate the considerable development you have achieved, midway through a project, when your own doldrums are likely to sink in. There is no other point in your voyage where both the start and the finish will be this far away from you. Investing in your morale and reassessing your progress is critical to remaining committed to the quest.

Teambuilding Lessons:

1. As a leader, you can sense a sudden slack in the team. It is as evident as a sail blowing out and forward momentum of a ship slowing. The easiest thing to do would be to ignore it, and let the team attend to the details of getting the sail down, sewn up, and hoisted aloft again. Taking this easy way out could be fatal to team morale, and is, I suspect, a major cause of project failure. A better approach would be to take the blown sail down, put it aside, hoist another functional sail and get moving again. Then call a summit meeting of all team members.

2. This momentum-addressing summit meeting begins with an acknowledgement that momentum may be stopped. Make the team understand that this is not only expected but also desirable. Every quest has its halfway point, and it is at that point that we are as far from both the beginning and end of the project as we will ever be. It would be superhuman to be as motivated as we were at the start. Offer to keep the project's basics on track yourself, and call a team hiatus. Let people have some off-time, even a day. In that time, ask them to update their skills inventory to reflect on all the new capabilities they have developed through the course of the project. Get ready for a second project kick-off.

Personal Development Worksheet #5

1. What are my instincts telling me right now about my quest?

2. What can I do in the coming week to confirm those instincts?

3. When will I get some time alone in the coming week? Where will I spend that time alone?

4. How have I changed, improved and developed over the past year?

Chapter 6:
Casting Off Again

A storm is forming quickly, and we have to weigh anchor and get moving again. Each sailor's reflections on the brief time spent ashore on Easter Island will have to wait. We hustle to get the anchor back up and the sails hoisted. We begin ghosting off as the skies turn a menacing steel grey colour, and cold air floods in to replace the muggy tropical heat. We are bound for the Roaring Forties, and later, the Furious Fifties of south latitude – arguably the most dangerous seas on the planet. This is what we have all come for, and we are both pumped and apprehensive at the same time. Of the now 30 crewmembers, only 4 have been down into the Southern Ocean, and – whether out of superstition, or deliberate myth-making – they don't talk about it. For most of us, this is the culmination of years spent reading and hearing about this place called the Southern Ocean. It is a place where many sailors have died, and those who have survived have earned some bragging rights.

Despite our "fear and loathing" surrounding the arrival of our new crew members on Easter Island, these additions proved to be very welcome to our pre-existing (and perhaps a bit stale?) crew. With no exceptions, each brought a unique set of skills and abilities to the table. Most were experienced sailors; there were two good riggers among them, a jumbo-jet pilot who was a weather expert, and one guy with an email-capable satellite phone, a gadget that sparked immediate lust among those of us hoping for some more contact with home. Rounding out the new additions were a documentary film-maker from England who would shoot our rounding of the Horn, a gracious tall ship veteran from California, and a German journalist who had been to every country in the world.

Why did these folks fit in so well, so fast? I think one of the reasons is that we needed new blood on our team. Yes, we had been through a fair amount, and friendships had formed. But so had irritations with one another. We were competent, but smug, and probably a bit complacent. We were getting boring.

The new crewmembers energized us all. We were excited to hear about their fascination with Cape Horn. They had new stories and legends to share. They had a hardcore fascination with being in the Southern Ocean and rounding the Horn that perhaps the rest of us had lost sight of, through aggravation, discomfort and routine. It picked us all up to have the original quest revisited and restated by fresh, clean, energized people – people who had done cool things like go for a bike ride or visit a supermarket in the last 2 months.

With a renewed sense of purpose, we sailed southwest toward the Horn. We were still not in the Roaring Forties, but the new crewmembers seemed to have brought the wind with them, and we had favourable winds from behind us, propelling us toward the Horn. Sailing was fairly easy given our skills and experience. We were doing well, and had appetite for more. We smiled a lot. We wondered when the 40s would start to roar...

The "Roaring Forties"

Around this time, we had a Halloween night, complete with "trick or treat" to remember a bit of our land culture. Anyone who showed up after watch with a costume was rewarded with a free glass of beer. Half the crew made an effort, and half thought it was stupid. I compromised, and put a cardboard shark fin on my head, downed the "treat", a free beer, and went to bed. A few hours later, the "tricks" began in the form of black squalls that would be our constant recurring companion for the next several weeks. All hands were ordered on deck: we had entered the Roaring Forties.

On the open Southern Ocean, a squall appears on the horizon as a black tube, extending from the clouds to the ocean. Despite the odds of them passing to either side of the ship, these squalls seemed to have a homing instinct, and inevitably engulfed us head-on. A squall usually results in strong gusts of wind, as well as rain or hail for around 20 minutes, and then it moves on. The wind increase is so dramatic that if a ship is caught unaware, it can be overwhelmed by wind and waves. A very real risk is blowing out all the sails while getting knocked-down, a situation that can be fatal if violent waves capsize the vessel while she is knocked-down. For this reason, we all needed to be very vigilant and scanning the horizon all the time.

We went into a squall watch mode. A squall that you see coming can be coped with, whereas one that surprises you can be deadly. It is always a hassle and a lot of work to drop all the sails, using many of the 200 lines on the ship, only to have to haul them back up in 20 minutes to avoid losing speed when the weather returns back to normal. In bad times, the squalls came every 45 minutes, and the work was backbreaking, fatiguing and demoralizing. Nonetheless, coping with the squalls was better than the alternative, so we just got better at it. More than once I went off-watch to bed, knowing that a squall was due in about 15 minutes, but realizing that the next watch would have to deal with it – thank goodness! If the squall was coming sooner than that, we generally stayed up longer and dealt with it ourselves, to spare the oncoming watch. I doubt I was the only one who watched the squall's approach and secretly hoped to be off-watch and in my rack when it hit.

The Roaring Forties, with their building seas and never-ending squalls, were rendering us all like new parents of a colicky baby. We wandered around like zombies, responding instantly and half-awake to crisis after crisis. Still, we were getting better at it, and we knew we couldn't crack now. We were too far away from land to be rescued, and the Furious Fifties promised to be even more extreme. In the best and worst senses of the word, we were committed.

Spiraling the Rig

As you look up the mast of a tall ship, there are a number of sails, hung from yards, one above the other. The sails get smaller as you go up. One of the most dangerous things that can happen at sea is that the sails get "backed" or end up oriented the wrong way to the wind. The same is true on a small, simple sailboat, where the boom can suddenly swing across and smack somebody in the head because the ship was steered across the wind, and the wind got onto the wrong side of the sail without warning. Most times, on a small boat, the result is a bruised head and ego. On a tall ship, with six or seven sails on each mast, the consequences of backing the sails can lead to dismasting and sinking. As a result, a system has evolved whereby the sails are "spiraled" from top to bottom. What this means is that the top sail, which is also the smallest, is angled further than the others into the wind. This way, if the helmsperson makes a mistake, they will see that smaller, top sail flog and get backed before the other sails get backed. This means they can steer back on course before anything serious happens. The worst that can happen is that the top sails may need to be loosened and brought back into alignment. This is much better that having all the sails get backed as the result of a brief lapse in attention to steering!

Spiraling the rig, then, is an early warning system. All teams need one. The leadership of the team needs to decide what signals and signposts will be visible before the project goes off-track, and ensure that the early-warning signs are communicated to everybody on the team. And everybody, at all levels, should feel they are in a position to shout out that the top sail is getting backed.

Personal Insights:

1. The point at which you feel most confident and accomplished is precisely the moment when you most need your next stretch. As soon as find yourself thinking, "this is not so bad", or "I have gotten really good at this", you should have already begun seeking your next growth opportunity. If you don't, you may find yourself overwhelmed by a new challenge, whether you saw it coming or not. On the ship, we were always careful to be checking ourselves and each other for overconfidence. The word we passed around quietly was "hubris": we must beware of hubris, because a lot of cocky people have been killed down here. And many more have died attempting to rescue the overconfident sailor.

2. Keep an open mind about new team members. They are rarely going to pose the threat you fear they might, and in fact will likely re-energize the quest you are on. Also, they need to look to you as a guide to learn the ropes, and help quell their own anxieties. Remember yourself at the outset of the project? This is the beginning of your own growth into leadership.

Teambuilding Lessons:

1. Revisit and restate the quest. After a brief team hiatus, it is essential to call everyone together and get the team refocused. This can be aided if new people have joined the project at the midway point. These new people will need the overall goals of the project explained to them, and a project re-launch meeting can be a good time to review for everybody what the successes have been to date, and what remains to be accomplished.

2. Bring in new blood. By now, the project should have an allure to those not involved. Open the door to new interest and let some new people on board. Make a couple of promotions. Let somebody off who has had enough, and may no longer be committed. If necessary, expand the mandate of the team to accommodate the new talent. The result will be a shifting-off of the low-momentum sandbar that the project has run aground on, and revitalized commitment to the project. Even the restating of the project goals done for the benefit of the newcomers will remind the longstanding members of the team

why they are there, especially after the brief project hiatus discussed in Chapter 5. This is the project re-launch.

3. Study the weather and know where you are in relation to the elements. Appoint a navigator. The role of navigator should be assigned within the team, either to one person or as a rotating role. This person is responsible for knowing where the team is on the map from beginning to end of the project. Like a ship's weather expert, the navigator also has the responsibility of "reading the weather" and being aware of potential developments that could help or hinder the team's progress toward its goal. By keeping track of early warning signals, the navigator can steer the team around trouble by virtue of seeing it coming rather than simply reacting to seemingly "sudden" conditions.

4. Set a squall watch. Have someone scanning the horizon at all times to anticipate the regular crises that are inevitable in a quest or project. Rotate this role through the entire team so that each member gets a sense of what to be looking for. Similarly, get everyone involved in dealing with these "squalls" so that the response to them becomes practiced and automatic.

Personal Development Worksheet #6

1. What does my quest look like now? How has it changed since I began planning it? Restate the quest.

2. What abilities do I have that am I too comfortable with?

3. What can I do in the coming week to stretch myself again?

4. What new person can I involve in my quest? What fresh energy will they bring?

5. How can I re-launch my quest after bringing on a new person?

Chapter 7:
The Worst Place on Earth

We are in the grips of a real southern ocean storm. The wind is shrieking and the sea is awash in streaks of foam; 25 to 35 foot seas are angry and confused. Seawater is filling the deck when waves break, and tons of water are pouring out through the scuppers, holes in side of the boat designed for this purpose. A couple of crewmembers have almost been washed out into the sea, some having their legs pulled back through the scuppers just in time. This is what we have all come to see and what we have all feared. Storms aren't fun – things break, boats get overwhelmed and sink, people get hurt and die. As Seth the First Mate said earlier: "Storms are only fun when you talk about them afterwards in the bar." We are near 54 degrees south latitude in the Furious Fifties, a couple of degrees north of where Cape Horn is, and it is right here that most people get into trouble.

For the last 12 hours, we have had all the doors, windows and hatches "dogged-down" which means that thick metal plates have been bolted over them so that breaking seas can't smash them out and fill the boat. There is only one way up on deck from our racks below, and that is through a tortuous set of metal stairs leading up into the bridge on the raised rear deck. Having just one way in and out of down below does 2 things: it limits the access the sea has to the interior of the boat, and provides a way of accounting for everybody by having us all pass through the same place. The rules have been modified again. Two people on the helm at all times, rotating as often as possible. The lookouts are to be stationed near the helm. Nobody goes forward of the rear deck. Everybody else just stands by and waits for instructions, while staying out of danger.

A saying from an offshore sailing instructor of mine comes back to me: "The thing with storms is that no matter how bad they are, they are almost always gone within 36 hours or so." We are a third of the way through. Even better, I'm on holiday next shift!

Holiday is a ritual that was instituted when we started to get into heavier offshore conditions, in recognition of the fact that we are all getting more susceptible to dangerous fatigue. Although the voyage was over three-quarters complete, the dangers mostly all lay in this last stretch, when sea conditions and fatigue could lead to mistakes. It was a simple concept. Each watch could spare two people per shift, provided everybody else worked a little harder. This meant that someone could rest for eight hours instead of the usual four, and could repair their bodies and minds with some much-needed sleep. The entire crew was always happy for whoever was about to have an extra shift off, especially if it was themselves.

The way the numbers worked out, it was approximately 3 days between a person's last holiday and their next. This was an amazing motivating factor. You came back off holiday rejuvenated and in a position to buoy the spirits of those who were tiring out. You became the embodiment of what they would soon feel like after their own holiday. As the shifts wore on, your own reserves depleted themselves, and you began to long for your next holiday. I had a set ritual for holiday that I was able to maintain throughout the last weeks of the voyage. Since eight hours sleep seemed then like a fantastic, almost wasteful amount, I would spend the first half-hour socializing with the off-watch folks. Then I would go to the ship's library, if conditions permitted, to write in my journal for an hour. Then off to my rack where I had one of the chocolate bars I had bought in Easter Island while reading for a half-hour. Then I would put out the light and sink into an inky deep sleep for a luxurious six hours.

I was really glad to be heading into holiday in the middle of our big storm, because it meant I could miss the mid-section, and be recharged enough to cope when I came on shift next. In short, I knew I was going to make it, which was a great feeling, and in part was a sign of how I had matured as a sailor. I no longer saw gloom and disaster in everything that was new and scary. As bad as the storm was, I could see it wasn't getting much worse, and had seen enough smaller storms to know that it would always seem worst just before it began to moderate. Although we had to take extreme precautions with this big storm, I had no doubts we would get through it. This was a triumphant feeling, and was the realization of one of my personal goals from the outset of the voyage. I was less fearful, and much more competent. I sank into my bunk to nurse some injuries from a fall earlier in which I had hurt my back and thought I had broken a finger. On this night, I skipped the usual ritual and went straight to bed, falling asleep in minutes. When I awoke, 25 foot seas had given way to 15 foot seas, and things were on the way back to normal.

A few days later, I was awakened from a deep sleep by someone shouting: "You can see Diego Ramirez off to port!" I leapt out of my rack, tumbling down the heeled-over cabin to smack headfirst into the door. No matter, I was thrilled. Diego Ramirez Islands lie to the southwest of Cape Horn, and we were going to pass south of them, as I had hoped we would. I had read about these islands at the

Haul Away!

end of the earth for years and it was a life's dream to actually see them. I rushed up on deck, and could have cried from the beauty of the sight of these islands, that were close enough to be able to see trees on.

Seeing Diego Ramirez meant that we were "in the pipe," and we had no choice but to round Cape Horn, whether in one piece or a thousand. The Southern Ocean flows from west to east through the narrow Drake Passage, with huge rolling swells and strong winds, and anything in the vicinity goes with it. The effect is like being in a toilet that has been flushed – you are going to end up on the other side no matter what. Twelve hours later, just before midnight, we rounded Cape Horn, and soon turned left, up into the Atlantic.

Diego Ramirez Islands at the end of the earth

Rob Duncan

It was an unforgettable experience to finally see Cape Horn in person. The Horn was terrifying, beautiful and majestic, and I was humbled to be near it. The Horn represents the fulcrum between the Pacific and the Atlantic oceans, but just as vividly, also represented the fulcrum between anticipation and letdown for me. We were all over the moon as we rounded this amazing waypoint on all our life's voyages: cigars were smoked, drinks toasted, and hugs exchanged. But immediately after rounding, I was haunted by a huge feeling of letdown. We were finished. We had accomplished what we had set out to do, and now it was over. There was the detail of getting safely to the Falklands, and we needed to be careful, but essentially it was over, and I was sad. There was more grieving to come, but for now: mission accomplished.

A Pudding is Lost off Cape Horn.

One time when we were close to Cape Horn, the starboard watch had been making pudding for everyone. We were short of supplies, and this was going to be a rare treat. At one point, the ship lurched off a big wave, and a drinking glass went flying and shattered into the pudding bowl. After careful examination, it was determined that only half the bowl had glass in it, and that around half the pudding could be salvaged carefully by spooning it into another bowl. The starboard watch felt responsible, and decided to forgo their share of the pudding so that we, the port watch, could have a full serving each.

The port watch refused the offer. We felt that we all should have a little bit of pudding, or nobody should have any. Everybody or nobody. After some protesting, the starboard watch agreed, and we all enjoyed a spoonful or two of the pudding. Hardly satisfying for anybody, but fair. It may seem like a minor thing, but after 65 days at sea, the symbolism was huge to us. Each of us taking less pudding was a way of saying it could have been any of us who were there went the glass broke into the pudding. We rely on each other too much to place blame on something any one of us could have done.

There is a teambuilding lesson here: rather than focus on what you personally are not getting, do with a little less all around to share out the work, the rewards, or the suffering.

Personal Insights:

1. Things are worst just before they get better. My old offshore instructor's message about storms may sound trite when applied to project life, but I have found that it holds true. Somewhere near the end of a project or quest, there is a point at which you will be overwhelmed, fed up, and wondering why you ever got involved. This means things are about to turn the corner into the home stretch. Take a "holiday," similar to the four-hour shifts-off on the *Europa*. You don't have to go to Hawaii for a week, just be human and miss a scheduled team meeting, or kick off early on a Friday and go look at boats, or whatever nurtures you. Say "no" to something. When you come back "on-watch" you will find that the situation will have moderated, the team will have coped without you, and you will have the energy to push the last distance to the goal.

2. Have an off day. Every once in awhile on a long sailing passage, there will be days when you can see objectively that everything is going well, but you are grumpy and out-of-sorts anyway. There may be an impromptu party happening on deck with people laughing and

having a great time, but all you want to do with your free time is retire to your bunk and hate the world. These are the off days. It is easy to get down on yourself about having a bad attitude, but I have found that it is better to be forgiving with yourself, and just take yourself out of the action as much as possible, while taking care not to get in the way of other people's fun. There will be days when you are on top of the world, and having a great time, and you will look around, see someone else having an off day and smile. For now, just hit the bunk, lay low and try to be philosophical about things.

3. The end of the project or quest can be the worst stage of all. There is often an overwhelming feeling of disappointment as the team's goals are achieved. This may take a while to set in, some time after the project wrap-up party perhaps. This feeling is a natural part of the project, and must be gone through in order to have extracted all you can from the experience. The satisfaction of achieving the goals of the quest is counterbalanced by the sadness that comes with the end of the team. Like any other passing, this one must be mourned, and is accompanied with its own, uncontrollable phases of grief that

are unique to each team. In order to close the loop on the project, you must allow this phase to happen.

Teambuilding Lessons:

1. Recognize that at some point near the seeming end of the project, people will be at their worst: exhausted, annoyed and fragmented. See this as a normal phase of the project, and publicly acknowledge it. Let team members know you see this as a natural phase that comes right before success. Don't ignore it or try to manage it away.

2. Institute small individual holidays. When the team can afford it least is precisely when the team members need it most. It doesn't have to be a week off, perhaps just a "meeting vacation" or an early day. Make it rotate and be a regular, predictable ritual that people can bank on, barring some catastrophic crisis.

3. Plan for the project to not end with the achievement of the goals, but rather, when the members have gone through grieving the dissolution of the team. You may be frustrated that the cheers and pats on the back soon give way to lethargy and depression. Let it go. The team needs to grieve its own demise,

and this must play out in its own way. Resist the temptation to just throw everybody into a new challenge.

4. Know when to be a coach and when to be a driver. There were times in our voyage, when all we needed was support, encouragement and recognition to function at our highest. There were also times when it was necessary to be driven hard to get functioning again. Situations such as boredom, complacency, or dangerous extreme conditions were all times when we benefited from shake-ups, changes in personnel and being ordered to do things – fast. Know which style is which, when to apply them, and practice.

5. Leaders have off days too. This is particularly true for team leaders, especially new ones. Let yourself have flaws without beating up on yourself. Be candid about your most obvious flaws, and try to be humorous in showing the team that you are aware of them. Similarly, team members should let new team leaders grow into their roles, mistakes, warts and all. Try to not be too quick to criticize every mistake of a growing leader. After all, if everything goes well, it will be you in that role someday.

6. Allow a post-storm repose. Knowing when to suspend routine after a crisis is an art form that team leaders should understand. After one big storm, all routine on the ship was suspended for a few hours just to let everyone sleep and catch their breath. After a while, it was interesting to watch as people who had been down below for some time began to poke their heads up top, looking to re-engage with the task of sailing the ship. Others, who perhaps had been more shaken by the storm, were able to keep sleeping. As I observed this, it occurred to me that people were being allowed to voluntarily re-engage with the team on their own timeframe, and that the ultimate re-engagement was much stronger due to the fact that people were choosing their own moment to rejoin the team. The lesson I took from this was that if a team is blindsided by a really unpleasant situation, it may be better to let things be in disarray for a while, once the "basics of life" have been taken care of, and allow the team a breather. Communicate clearly that "we need a breather, let's pick it up tomorrow" (or Monday, or whatever is long enough for respite but not so long as to lose focus entirely). Some people will stay at it, some will take advantage

of the rest; all will come back feeling as though they have re-engaged, and on their own terms.

Personal Development Worksheet #7

1. What is the lowest point I have experienced on my quest?

2. What happened after the lowest point to make things seem better?

3. How will I take regular "holidays" during my quest? What rituals will bring me comfort?

4. What milestone will symbolize success in my quest?

5. How will I feel when after the milestone is achieved?

Chapter 8:
Journey's End

We are a couple of hours from dropping the hook in Port Stanley, Falkland Islands. We can see people and sheep on the shore. This is journey's end at last. We rounded Cape Horn several days ago, and are itching to get ashore and celebrate. I am sitting in the deckhouse with several crewmembers and the Captain when suddenly the ship is laid on her side by what later turned out to be a microburst – a freak weather event that takes the form of a severe squall that comes without warning. The deck is blue with huge hail pellets as the vessel rights herself and we scramble to get the few remaining sails down. Just as quick as it came, the freak wind passes, and the sun comes out.

Was that microburst Mother Nature's way of reminding us that she was in charge? Who knows? One thing is certain: it came at a point of cockiness and overconfidence, bringing our earlier warnings about hubris to mind. Fortunately we had had almost all the sails down in anticipation of motoring the last few hundred feet to drop the anchor. Otherwise our story might have ended very differently. As it turns out, nobody was hurt, and damage was minor. And it served us all well as a swift kick in the pants for a crew of newly minted Cape Horners who were frothing at the mouth to party.

Port Stanley had heard we were coming, and rolled out the welcome mat. The Globe Tavern adopted us as their own and showed us a fantastic party the first night we landed. For a crew of wobbly sailors who had been offshore for almost three months, it didn't take much to get us well-lubricated and dancing the night away.

The Europa viewed from a Cape Horner's grave in the Falklands

Haul Away!

My next few days were spent in stunned agony as the reality of my impending separation from my crewmates sank in. The *Europa* was going to sail on; most of us were getting off the boat in the Falklands; we were all flying back home, to different homes. We had become like a huge family, and the *Europa* had been our floating village. We spent day and night together, told stories, baked bread, weathered storms, and watched the sun rise and set day after day. The coming separation felt to me like being blown up by grenade into a dozen fragments.

Rob Duncan

A Gold Earring at the End of the Voyage

There is a rite of passage associated with rounding Cape Horn under sail that permits sailors to wear a gold earring in their left ear once they have rounded the Horn successfully. The tradition dates back several centuries to when sailors were required to wear gold on them to pay for their burial if they were washed overboard and onto shore near the Horn, which happened far too often. On our voyage, several of us had made a plan to observe this ritual, and we had talked about it and joked about it often on night watches and other quiet occasions. The gold earring became a powerful symbol of the milestone we were trying to achieve. The day after we rounded the Horn, several new earrings had appeared, and the captain said simply at our "2 O'Clockie" meeting: "Those gold earrings look good on you." Nothing more was said, but the symbolism was strong: we had achieved our team goal. Even the staunch "I never wear jewelry" guys were looking at the new hardware, and rubbing their earlobes thoughtfully between their fingers.

As a team, it is important to establish a victory symbol: a thing, a ritual, or some sort of event that will define and mark success. The symbol can be a party, or an engraved knick-knack – it doesn't matter. The key is not what the actual symbol is physically – let the team decide that – but that the symbolism itself is shared with all members of the team, and then honored upon reaching the team's goals.

Haul Away!

Personal Insights:

1. The more highly-functioning the team, and the more difficult the quest, the more painful it is to disband afterwards and let the team die. We see this time after time when ballplayers finally get their World Series ring and then never see the same heights again. It is important to anticipate that this is coming, and not try to manage your way around the feelings that will inevitably happen. Let yourself feel the letdown, but don't dwell on it excessively. Feel it when it comes over you, acknowledge it, and let it go for a while. You will go through stages of grieving not unlike when a pet dies, or you lose your job. These feelings don't detract from what you accomplished. They will fade over time, particularly when the team is ready to reconnect and say farewell. For my Cape Horn crewmates and me this happened months later in France, when we all got together again, effectively to say farewell.

Teambuilding Lessons:

1. Have a rite of passage like a wrap-up party with certificates, paperweights or other memento of the team's achievement.

2. Have a way for the team members to stay in touch. Within a small company or department, this can be as simple as a get together a few months later. With a more far-flung team, it can be an email distribution list or online bulletin board. Let the team members drive the timing. They will be sick of each other at first, and also let down by the end of the quest.

Personal Development Worksheet #8

1. How will I keep the members of my team in touch with each other after the project is finished?

2. What will our shared symbol of achieving our goal be?

3. When and where will we meet for a post-dissolution get-together?

4. What will my next quest be? (Re-use this book's Personal Development Worksheets as needed – and good luck!)

Chapter 9:
Epilogue

It has been 6 months since we rounded the Horn, and I am running down an unfamiliar cobblestone street in St. Malo, France, from my hotel toward the harbour. The Europa is in the harbour, and I can see the tips of her masts as I get closer. It is around 10pm, and the ship looks deserted, but I know that someone will be on watch on deck. The gangplank is roped off to prevent tourists from wandering onboard now that it is night-time. My heart is pounding as I undo the rope and walk up onto the ship's deck. In the darkness I spot a crewmate and break into a big smile. "Permission for a Cape Horner to come aboard?" "Permission granted!" he answers. We embrace.

For months after the completion of our rounding of Cape Horn, it was as if radio silence had been imposed on the crew. Despite free and easy access to email, it was a long time before I

Haul Away!

heard from any of them, or felt like reaching out myself. I was to learn afterwards, that virtually all of us who went back to our lives after Cape Horn fell into a bit of a funk, some worse than others. For me, there was an immense feeling of pride, and of having grown. I felt I had been successful in changing those aspects of my make-up that I hadn't been happy with. I was much less fearful of change and danger, and had a much healthier appetite for risk. I was also proud to have achieved a number of my life's goals. But at the same time, there was a huge sense of disappointment, and of loss. We had achieved something very special, that few others had done, and yet there was this nagging sense of despair and despondency: the team had been allowed to die, and all that had been special about it had been allowed to stop. We had stepped outside the boundaries of ordinary life, and had now stepped back in.

I did a few talks and slide shows about the voyage, wrote an article and started this book, but couldn't pull myself out of the feeling that I had betrayed myself on some level by coming back, and that the team had died without a valid reason. I was very happy to be home and back teaching, but there was some unfinished business lurking in the background. I needed closure. I decided to go to Saint-Malo.

Saint-Malo, in the Brittany region of France, is a beautiful medieval walled city that is steeped in maritime history. The city was to be the site of the last-ever meeting of the original Cape Horners who had sailed around the Horn on square-rigged cargo ships during the age of sail. The members of this near-secret society had been meeting periodically since 1937 in far-flung locations like Valparaiso, Chile and Turku, Finland. Once numbering thousands of sailors, their numbers had thinned to around 150, with an average age somewhere in the 70s or 80s. Struck by the frequency of deaths among their ranks, they had decided to hold one final meeting as an international group, and then disband. As the scant literature about the meeting noted, they wished their society to "die in beauty and dignity", rather than just continue to trail off through attrition.

It no doubt came as a bit of a surprise to these old-timers when a few of we recent Cape Horners ferreted out the necessary email addresses and began to enquire about the possibility of joining their final meeting. It had long been planned that the *Europa* would be stopping in the harbour at Saint-Malo, on its way back to Holland, during this last Cape Horners meeting to provide a kind of historical backdrop for the festivities. But it was equally clear to the vessel and her crew that this was not a meeting that we were welcome to infiltrate. Our presence was appreciated, but out on the dock, not in the more private festivities on land.

Despite this initially forbidding exterior, which I completely understood, a few of us persisted and through the graciousness of the group's leader, the "Great Mast" Roger Ghys, we secured invitations to participate. Captain Ghys felt it was appropriate since we had rounded the Horn in the traditional way, from 50 degrees south in one ocean, to 50 degrees south in the other ocean, entirely under sail on a square-rigger. It had been a few weeks since I had received the invitation, but I was ambivalent about going, since I was getting comfortably ensconced in home life again, and felt greedy about taking off again so soon.

Nevertheless, it dawned on me that I had to go, in order to give our voyage a context both historically and personally. It was also a chance to see many of my crewmates again for the first time since we split up. The more I thought about it, the more I realized it was my destiny to go there. The voyage wasn't finished otherwise, and that nagging feeling of disappointment wasn't going to go away until I closed the loop.

Cape Horners old and young gathered in Saint-Malo

Rob Duncan

I arrived in Saint Malo in the early evening, and took a taxi to my hotel from the train station. Rounding the corner toward the old part of the city, I could see the *Europa*'s three masts in the harbour, and my heart sang. We drove past, and I scoured her in vain for signs of my crewmates. My hotel turned out to be a few blocks away, and I ran the entire distance down to the ship after throwing my bags into my room.

A few minutes later I arrived out of breath at the gangplank, which was chained off for the night from the public. I undid the chain, and spying one of my crewmates said: "Permission for a Cape Horner to come aboard?" The rest was fantastic. A wonderful whirl of hugs and catching up ensued. We were all genuinely happy to see one another again, and I could immediately feel the closure I had been craving. It got even better over the coming days, when I was invited to raise the Canadian flag at the Cape Horners memorial ceremony, and we got to spend time with the older generations of Cape Horners, who were gracious and full of stories.

The subject of new challenges came up a few times during this reunion visit, and it is something I still reflect on. We talked about sailing the *Europa* from east to west, the "wrong way" around the Horn, and there was some interest in that one. I have thought about sailing my own little boat, "Mischief II," offshore, perhaps as far as Hawaii. In the meantime, now that I am back from Saint-Malo, I am at peace with the voyage, and have

Haul Away!

Albatross statue at the Cape Horner's Museum, near Saint-Malo

the warmest place in my heart for my crewmates. Perhaps some of us will sail together again, perhaps not. It doesn't matter, not in the same heart-rending way it seemed to matter after Cape Horn. Now the circle is closed and the voyage has its rightful place in the context of our lives. The main thing is we got it done. We really did it, Cape Horners all.

Appendix One:
On Being a Leader

An Interview with Klaas Gaastra, Captain of the Tall Ship *Europa*, Atlantic Ocean, July 10, 2004.

Background: In June 2004, I re-joined the tall ship Europa to sail from France to Nova Scotia, across the Atlantic Ocean. Klaas Gaastra was the captain on the voyage. I mentioned to him that I was writing a teambuilding book that had been inspired by our earlier voyage around Cape Horn. I asked if I could interview him, and he graciously agreed. The interview took place on night watch, at around 2am in the pilothouse of the Europa. I had come to the interview with 5 questions in mind, as reflected below.

1. What is your greatest challenge as a leader? How do you manage/approach this challenge?

The biggest challenge is that sometimes you have to disrupt the teambuilding efforts that have been working previously. An example is when someone's flight schedule forces a delay in the ship's arrival or departure times and dates. These things can get very frustrating for everybody. Think back to Easter Island on our Cape Horn voyage. We were very late getting there, and were forced to detour off a good course to get there to pick up the other crewmembers. It was a tense situation for everybody. What you have to do is "open the valve" and let the tension out, let people speak up and voice their concerns and frustrations. That's what the "2 O'Clockie" meeting is good for.

2. The "2 O'Clockie" seems like a great management tool for hearing about potential team problems. How did this tradition evolve, and how does it help you as a leader?

It just happened. Sea watches make it really hard to get everybody all together at the same time, and yet, if you don't do something about that, tensions can grow unchecked. This is how the "2 O'Clockie" came about. It at least gives everybody a chance to speak out and voice any concerns they have. Some speak up, and some

Haul Away!

don't, but at least they have all had the chance. It's much better than having a discussion "at the bar" because the alcohol affects the atmosphere. This way, everyone gets called on to voice any concerns they have in a neutral setting. Some people choose not to express themselves at that time. Sometimes they try to engage me privately, at which point I can say: "That's a great item for the "2 O'Clockie". After a while everybody knows that 2pm is the appointed time to bring things up, every day.

The "2 O'Clockie" is also a time for me to inform people, to let them know the factors and decisions that I am facing. I can share those with everybody and get their ideas. In the end, I'm the one who has to decide, but this way I don't look like a dictator. Besides, there's an art to having the crew feel as though they are the ones coming up with the decisions, even if they are the decisions I would have made anyway (laughs)!

3. How do you take a group of strangers and build them into an effective team?

You have to work to bring out the best in each person. Every person has something good in them. You need to encourage everyone to feel proud of the ship and all of the teams' successes – even if it is just a good round of peeling potatoes!

> *4. What advice would you give to someone who wants to be a good team member? A good team leader?*

A sense of humour is key to being a good team member. Keep a sense of perspective on yourself and what is going on. If possible, try to see yourself as smaller relative to the larger picture of what is happening on board the ship. Don't get annoyed with other people. Learn what your own triggers are with particular people and try to see your irritation coming. Use humour to defuse the situation.

As a leader, a sense of humour is also key. You also need to keep your eyes and ears open, and be alert to the things that are likely to trigger tensions in the crew, A couple of years ago, we were in a fog for 2 solid weeks. This made our world very small, and everyone felt lumped together and tensions started to rise. As a leader, if I can anticipate this coming, I can use things like humour to help make the situation easier to live with. The triggers are often bad weather, rain, thunder, lightening, that sort of thing. Generally you can anticipate the tension rising.

Leadership isn't something you can learn by taking a class. Experience is the best teacher; you have to learn by doing. Often leaders emerge in difficult situations, especially if the person can stay calm, keep a good overview of the situation, and delegate where possible. Remember that the leader is in the minority, so you need to motivate people to do things without seeming like a dictator. Part of that is keeping everybody informed.

I personally never "sought command." I started in a small boat, where you are the skipper by default. Over time, the boats got bigger, I got older and my experience grew. You can see who might make a good leader, though. Some people come aboard and you sense that they will be colleagues and captains in their own right in a few years. Others, you know it just won't happen. It has to do with an ability to motivate people, as well as maintaining a sense of humour, keeping everyone's spirits up.

5. What is your greatest satisfaction as a leader, as Captain?

The greatest satisfaction for me is seeing people come back on board the ship again for a second or third time. A lot of people say that their time on the ship was a turning point in their lives. It feels great to know that the experience we provided on the ship made a difference in people's lives. I think a tall ship offers a unique opportunity to get away from modern life, with its TV, isolation and constant news, and share life with others for 24 hours a day. It's interesting to be able to show people that they can in fact live without the "privacy" they claim to need in modern life. People on a ship can experience really deep team bonds and a sense of having pride in what they are able to do, both for the ship and for themselves.

Appendix Two:
Motivational Teambuilding Seminars by Rob Duncan

The author, Rob Duncan, is available to speak to audiences on the themes of teambuilding, and achieving great goals. Drawn from the lessons contained in this book and elsewhere, Rob's seminars can be custom-designed for your group or organization. A variety of lengths and formats are possible, including keynote addresses, lunch & learns, half-day and full-day seminars, with a variety of interactive exercises and take-away materials.

Presented in story and full-color photographs, the messages in Rob Duncan's motivational teambuilding seminars will leave your crew feeling empowered and capable of achieving all their goals, both organizational and personal.

Participants have had this to say:

> *"An excellent and most inspiring presentation!"*

> *"The parallel of sailing and teamwork – loved it!"*

> *"This was a great presentation! Wonderful theme and a very good presenter – great pictures!"*

To learn more about these uplifting seminars, please visit Great Capes, Rob's company, at www.greatcapes.com. Contact information is included on the website, and we would be delighted to discuss your specific needs with you.

About the Author

In 2002, management consultant and college instructor Rob Duncan sailed as a deckhand on the tall ship Europa on an 8,000 mile voyage around the dreaded Cape Horn. In doing so, Rob joined an exclusive group of fewer than 500 living people to have rounded the Horn on a square-rigged sailing ship. An account of the voyage appeared in Pacific Yachting magazine in 2003. Rob Duncan holds a BA in Economics, an MBA and is a Certified Management Consultant. Through his company, Great Capes Consulting (www.greatcapes.com), Rob offers motivational teambuilding seminars and keynote addresses. When he is not consulting or teaching, Rob can often be found on his own sailboat in the Pacific Northwest.

Printed in the United States
27420LVS00002B/388-459